D1448846

Take Charge of Your Career!
365 Tips, Tricks, and Techniques to Achieve Happiness at Work and in Life

Karin Ireland

Course Technology PTR
A part of Cengage Learning

COURSE TECHNOLOGY
CENGAGE Learning

Australia, Brazil, Japan, Korea, Mexico, Singapore, Spain, United Kingdom, United States

© 2012 Karin Ireland.

For product information and technology assistance, contact us at
Cengage Learning Academic Resource Center, 1-800-354-9706.

For permission to use material from this text or product,
submit all requests online at **cengage.com/permissions.**
Further permissions questions can be emailed to
permissionrequest@cengage.com.

All trademarks are the property of their respective owners.

Library of Congress Catalog Card Number: 2011942186

ISBN-13: 978-1-4354-6095-9

ISBN-10: 1-4354-6095-2

Course Technology, a part of Cengage Learning
20 Channel Center Street, Boston, MA 02210, USA

Cengage Learning is a leading provider of customized learning solutions with office locations around the globe, including Singapore, the United Kingdom, Australia, Mexico, Brazil, and Japan. Locate your local office at **international.cengage.com/region.**

Cengage Learning products are represented in Canada by Nelson Education, Ltd. For your lifelong learning solutions, visit **courseptr.com.**
Visit our corporate website at **cengage.com.**

Printed in the United States of America
1 2 3 4 5 6 7 13 12 11

For Francis, who always believes in me,
and for Tricia, who was there.

Karin Ireland has been a writer for more years than she'd like to admit, and spent many of them working for other people. She passes along what she learned the hard way and hopes you will be quicker to balance who you are with what you do so you'll have a smoother journey.

It's easier to be happy when you don't spend time thinking about the reasons you aren't.

Spend time with people who get things done instead of people who complain about how hard something is to do or why it can't be done.

Nothing changes after you say, "Yes, but…" Instead, say, "Okay, and so…" Then think about possibilities. Ask yourself, *What if…?*

You can always be the boss—of you. Your boss can make you do certain tasks at work, but only you can choose how you respond and how you feel.

Never tell a coworker something you have to make her promise not to repeat.

People who don't like surprises like to control everything. If your boss is a controller, try to avoid surprises.

Sometimes a decision is as easy as flipping a coin. Disappointed with the result? You have your answer: You wanted the other choice.

Make yourself known to the decision makers in your department, division, company. Sometimes it's easier to lay off people who aren't known.

You can't change your boss or your coworkers. If they're crazy and you can't leave, imagine you're in an episode of *The Office*, and you're an actor. Then play the role you're being paid to play.

Note to the workaholic: Just because you can check your work voice mail or email at 11:30 p.m. and on weekends doesn't mean you should. Try to say no to that voice that always pushes you to do more. Your mind and body need rest.

In a conflict, listen first. Confirm the points you agree on before you try to convert others to your way of thinking.

Before you speak, know the result you want and what you need to say or do to get it.

Don't close any doors at an interview. The only time you need to decide whether you want the job is after it's offered.

Sometimes people buy a product or an idea because it's what they want; other times they buy because of how it makes them feel. Whatever you sell (an idea or a product), look for ways to help people feel good about saying yes.

If you work at a company where you can't be honest and honor your integrity, look for a new job right away.

Unless there's a lion chasing you, don't make decisions based on fear.

Job interviewers will judge you by your email address. Make sure yours reflects the image you want it to. *OneHotMama* and *KillerDude* aren't who employers are looking for.

When there's a conflict, stop and ask yourself, *What would an impartial observer say is going on?* Then ask yourself, *What would an impartial observer suggest I do next?*

Put your work down and give your boss, your spouse, or your children your full attention when they want to talk to you. Many who have thought their work was more important have woken up one day without a job, a spouse, or children.

Ask your boss for feedback every three months. It shows you're interested in being a valuable employee.

Avoid being pulled into gripe sessions. Remember a deadline, excuse yourself, and look for other ways to bond with people.

Think of your job as a game. Do the best you can; then go home and do something different.

Delete, file, or act on emails right away rather than letting them pile up and get lost in the queue.

Resisting change is like trying to play baseball while refusing to let go of the football from an earlier game. You won't win.

Spelling and grammar matter, even in the shortest, most casual emails.

If your boss or other executive wants to boast, let him. He'll be more generous when he's feeling pleased with himself than if you show him you're not impressed.

Don't let your job take all your energy or all your time. Work is an important part of your life, but be sure it's only a part.

Meditate. It really does help. Follow your breath or your heartbeat. Let tight muscles relax.

Avoid the temptation to push people deeper into anger. It won't lead to a positive resolution, and it can be dangerous.

If you're not getting what you want by doing what you're doing, figure out what you need to change: your job? your friends? your work habits? your attitude? Then change it.

Try not to accept a job until you've met your
boss and an employee or two and you've walked
through the work area to see how you feel there.
Notice whether people look relatively happy.

Relationships are important. When you're with
other people, *be* with them—not checking your
iPhone for messages, the weather, the latest
news, or sports scores.

Find ways to be your own security blanket.
Live where you can afford to live, buy what you
can afford to buy, and save some money so you
won't have to worry about unexpected expenses.

Know who runs your company and what their goals are. Know who runs your division and your department and what their goals are. Then figure out what you can do to help them reach their goals.

Look for ways to be happy.

If others don't seem to be paying attention to your presentation, say, "I think I've lost you; can you tell me where that happened?" Then look for another way to make your message relevant to them.

Get enough sleep. Accidents, mistakes, bad moods, and bad health happen when people are sleep deprived.

If you're the boss, make it safe for your employees to tell you the truth.

People who are rude may not be angry with you—they might just be having a bad day/week/year. Don't let others make you unhappy.

Don't exaggerate; it makes people question the accuracy of other things you say.

Before an interview, practice answering the question, "Where do you see yourself in five years?" Research the company. Do managers expect employees to stay in one department for life? Are managers eager to hire employees who want to advance? Where *do* you see yourself in five years?

Stand up when people come to your work space, and they won't stay as long.

Respect the cultural preferences of people from other countries. If you don't know what they are, ask someone who does.

No matter what you think of your boss, she's smart enough to be in a higher position than you are. Look for something to learn from her, and remember to breathe.

Instead of stressing to figure things out, slow down so you can notice your own inner guidance.

Follow a few blogs that share helpful tips on workplace success. Don't read them at work, though.

When you begin a sentence with, "You probably know that..." you give your listener credit for being informed, and he'll be more inclined to listen to what comes next.

Be willing to walk away (kindly) from people and situations that aren't good for you.

Even the best employees are sometimes let go. Know your company's competitors and how you might fit in, and keep your resume up to date.

Ask a potential boss how she decides if an employee is doing a good job. Listen carefully. If she can't be specific, she won't be able to help you be the kind of employee she values.

Slow down. Take your breaks. Life isn't about seeing how fast you can get everything done. Have you noticed that once you do finish a list there's already another one that's just as urgent?

People judge nervousness as a liability. Stop biting or picking your fingernails. Don't crack your knuckles when others are around. If you bounce your foot or your leg when you're sitting, stop it.

When you go to your boss with a problem, have a couple of solutions to offer, too.

The stories you tell yourself can help make you happy and successful, or they can help keep you stuck. Practice telling yourself stories that are about what you *can* do instead of what you *can't*.

Say "no" more often. You probably don't have to do a lot of the things you think you have to do.

Proofread your emails before you click Send. Are they specific enough so your readers know exactly what you intend to say? Are there enough soft words so the message doesn't sound angry or bossy? Are you clear if you expect readers to take action? Are your punctuation and grammar correct?

Get to work on time. Get to meetings on time. Go home on time.

Understand your company's 401(k) plan, and
take advantage of it.

Don't finish people's sentences. Sometimes they
aren't going to say what you think they are.

If you *really* want the job, don't try to bond
with the interviewer by commenting fondly
on the pictures of children on her desk. Many
companies believe employees with children will
want too much time off, and the pictures could
be a trick to see if you'll say you have kids.

Every company has policies that seem ridiculous or unfair. Every company has bosses who are clueless. You probably won't be able to change them, but you can change how much you let it bother you.

Practice by interviewing for one or two jobs you don't care about before interviewing for ones you do.

Don't chew gum at work. People watching will mentally lower your IQ by about twenty points.

Ask yourself, *What one belief keeps me from doing what I long to do?* Then ask, *How can I let that belief go?*

Don't expect to be able to do two people's jobs without eliminating half the work. If your boss insists you must do it all, do what you reasonably can, and look for another job.

Do what successful people are doing, not what unsuccessful people say you should do.

Pay attention to messages from your body. Constant headaches, backaches, and stomach aches can warn you that you're under too much stress. Don't just accept the fact that you're stressed. Find ways to decrease or eliminate it.

Introduce yourself if others forget to introduce you.

Turn off your personal cell phone during interviews and meetings with your boss or other important people at work.

Many organizations aren't looking for workers who are brilliant; they're looking for people who will do a good job without causing trouble.

The best way to have a loyal employee is to be a loyal boss.

At work, don't act on your first impulse, and don't offer the first response that comes to mind. If your idea is sound when you think of it, it will be sound after you've had time to explore it some.

Be willing to put in the effort to work well with others.

Don't help your boss say what she's saying. You may think you're being supportive, but she'll think you're annoying.

Every day do five specific things that move you toward reaching your most important goal.

Avoid approaching others with the intent of pushing your agenda through. Instead, ask questions and work for win/win results.

Ask a potential boss how success is rewarded. Pay attention to his answer. Do you believe him?

Listen to motivational and self-help CDs on the way to and from work instead of the news.

Ask yourself often, *Is what I'm doing taking me where I want to go?*

Don't make people guess what you want. Tell them.

Networking is more about farming than hunting. It's possible to make great connections on the first meeting, but be willing to put time into developing relationships.

We're *supposed* to be different. Enjoy the different ways other people look, think, and behave.

The highest incidence of heart attacks is said to be Monday at 9 a.m. Plan something that will make you happy on all your Monday mornings.

Long for your own business? Practice now. Think of your boss and your coworkers as customers. Would they choose to do business with you if they didn't have to?

Don't tell coworkers how you did it at your last job.

If your company is experiencing serious financial difficulties, it might be time to start looking for another job.

Remember to breathe. Relax. Play.

Don't listen to the dream stealers. There are always people who are certain that what you want to accomplish won't work. What they really mean is that it won't work *for them*.

Follow a job interview with a thank-you note. Write a draft first. Use words that make you sound excited about working at that company, and make sure you spell all the words correctly. Be sure to spell the interviewer's name and title correctly, too.

If you're a supervisor, look for ways to make employees glad they work for you. Help your company find ways to make all employees glad they work for your company.

Determine a reasonable quitting time and stick to it. If you're regularly working several hours late, look for ways to be more efficient, look for ways to minimize distractions, and look for tasks you might not really need to do.

Safety can be hazardous to your health if you stay at a safe job that is making you ill.

Avoid judging others. Many people live with challenges no one knows about. Ultimately, everyone wants acceptance, approval, and love. Some just have an unappealing way of asking for it.

No matter how busy you are, don't let your boss or your customers feel like they're interrupting you.

Every day, do something that makes you feel happy.

Every day, do something to make someone else happy.

Win your boss's confidence by being responsible and positive, meeting deadlines, and keeping her informed of your progress.

Avoid blaming others for your mistakes, but don't blame yourself harshly, either. You'll never be perfect; just try not to make the same mistake more than once or twice.

Work to find an agreeable solution, not to win your point.

Ask yourself regularly, *Does the work I'm about to do have to be done? Does it have to be done by me? Does it have to be done perfectly, or is just finishing it okay?*

The happier your boss is, the happier you'll be. Do what you can to keep your boss happy.

Surround yourself with people who look for solutions rather than people who look for problems.

Don't wait to be told to do things you know need to be done.

Don't insist on always having the last word.

If you're stressed, don't escape into TV, video games, online chat groups, alcohol, or other mind-numbing activities. Instead, look for a fun hobby you can do with others, or find a place to volunteer where you'll feel valuable.

Wait until you're sure of your facts before you offer them.

Don't stay in a job that forces you to do or be anything you're not comfortable doing or being.

What your boss thinks about you personally may be more important than what she thinks about your work. Always show her the best version of yourself.

Ask yourself frequently, *What is the easiest way to do what I'm about to do that will still bring good results?*

Focus on the parts of your job that are good. Try to enjoy something about even the most boring or difficult task.

Be grateful—not just for the material things you have, but for the people who are in your life, for your health, for the freedom to take charge of your life.

You'll be happier if you remember the difference
between what you want and what you need.

Find a way to manage clutter on your desk.
One way is to make lists of projects and ideas
you don't want to forget about; then forget about
them until you check your list the following day
or week.

Practice relying more on yourself and less on
others. Look for ways to reduce dependency on
your job. Pay off debts, and avoid taking on
new ones.

Stay out of office gossip. Always have something interesting in mind you can offer to redirect a conversation.

When you need to apologize, do it right away, and do it sincerely. The person you're apologizing to may not accept gracefully. Let that be okay.

You are never going to be as important at work as you think you should be. Let that be okay.

Listen to what people are trying to say, as well as to what they are saying. Ask questions to get more information.

If you're the boss, make it safe for your staff to contribute ideas.

Expect your coworkers to work as a team, but don't be frustrated if they don't. Look for ways to make them want to be part of the team.

Moving stuff around isn't the same as getting stuff done.

Martial arts and high-energy dance classes can help eliminate stress while you're having fun.

Keep learning about your job, your boss's goals, your organization's goals, your competitors, your industry. Take workshops, and go back to school if it will help you be a more valuable employee.

Make your goals more about how you want to feel than what you want to have.

If your mind wanders during meetings, take notes. It doesn't matter whether you'll read them again; the process will help you pay attention, and some of the information will stick.

After meetings you lead, send an email to participants that lists the plans of action that were agreed on and decisions that were made.

Don't change who you are, but consider
changing the way you do certain things if it
will make your boss happy.

Don't change who you are in order to be liked,
but do look for ways to be the best you that
you can.

Try to understand the fear that keeps you from
doing what you want or need to do. Ask yourself,
*Whose stories am I listening to (a parent's? the
media's?) about what's safe and what isn't?*

Help people understand what you're saying.
Organize your thoughts as if you were writing
a memo with a clear beginning, middle, end,
and request for what you want.

Do work that will bring you positive recognition
before you do work that's merely routine or easy.

Know when it's better to speak up or keep
quiet; ask for help or try one more thing; offer
help, or wait and see.

During a job interview or at meetings, avoid crossing your arms or showing boredom, impatience, or disgust. Soften the muscles in your face; make eye contact, but don't stare.

Know what you really want. If you discover you're on the wrong path, get off as soon as possible. Change gets harder the longer you wait.

Life is not a challenge for you to attempt to get more work done than anybody else. Take time to look for ways to be happy.

Ask yourself, *What would I do differently if I knew failure was often just a bump in the road and not a cliff?*

Act on those urges to do something nice for your coworkers: give a compliment, send a card, pass along a compliment or a funny cartoon.

Figure out how to be organized. Buy a book, go to a workshop, do whatever it takes. Nothing will waste your time or make others doubt your value more than missing deadlines or losing paperwork because you aren't organized.

You don't have to do everything by yourself. Be willing to ask for help. If you're in an environment where you can't ask for help, you should probably consider leaving.

If your primary projects are eliminated and aren't replaced by others, it might be time to start looking for another job.

Every behavior sends a message. Your behavior might not send the message you intend, so if people surprise you with their response, ask for feedback.

It's hard to recognize that you're overworking while you're overworking. Plan regular breaks to get up and walk around. Notice the areas of your body that are tight—your shoulders, neck, stomach—and relax them. Breathe.

Work for applause from yourself, not from others.

Notice what doesn't work at your company, and don't do it.

The secret to effective networking is to first find out how you can help others.

A promotion is a new job. Before you say yes, know what the new duties are, how you feel about them, and how the promotion will improve your life, not just your paycheck.

Look for ways to do a good job with less effort and time.

Don't try *too* hard to be likeable. It makes people uncomfortable.

If your ideas conflict with the agendas of more powerful people at your company, they won't be considered. See how you can tweak your ideas so they will help the powerful people reach their goals.

Right or wrong, people judge you by what you wear, the way you talk, and what you talk about.

When you focus on what you don't want instead of what you do, it's like rehearsing for a play you don't want to be in.

Your health is more important than your job. If your job jeopardizes your health, look for a new one right away. Hush those voices that tell you why you can't leave or shouldn't leave...and find a way to leave.

If there is widespread talk of restructuring your department and reclassifying positions, it might be time to start looking for another job.

Make feeling successful about who you are, not about your job title, house, or car.

Ask yourself often, *How would the person I want to be say or do what I'm about to say or do?*

Ask the interviewer how she sees your experience meeting the needs of your potential boss. Let her sell herself on you as a good match.

Have a friend question you in a mock interview
before the real one. You'll be surprised how
much you'll stumble until you've practiced.

Listen your way into the insiders' group. If you
tell them how much *you* know, you won't find
out how much *they* know, and you need to
know what they know to move ahead.

Look for ways to have fun on a budget: Buy or
rent CDs and DVDs of concerts instead of going
in person; invite friends over to watch special
programs on TV; find fancy hotels where you
can have lunch instead of paying for an
overnight stay.

Be the person you'd like other people to be.

Challenge yourself to find ways not to let a crazy boss make you crazy.

Don't fool yourself into believing you'll change your stressful life as soon as you reach a certain goal. By the time you get close to it, you'll have another goal you'll think you have to wait for.

Take frequent breaks. Don't always work as hard as you can. Being a workaholic isn't healthy, and it won't make you happy.

If you ask for help, be sure to ask the right person the right question in the right way.

Proofread. Proofread. Proofread. If upper management or the public will see what you've written, ask someone else to proofread it, too.

Your attitude can be the difference between keeping your job and being let go.

If anyone has reached the goal you have in mind, chances are you can, too. You just have to figure out how.

Learn to listen to what a person is saying, not what you think he's saying or what you'll say when he takes a breath.

Be curious before being angry. When you find out what's really going on, you might not feel angry anymore.

If speaking to a group makes you nervous, join Toastmasters. If you suspect your grammar isn't flawless, take a class so it is.

Develop a good handshake. Ask for feedback, and practice until you get it right.

Forgive people who have hurt you—not for
their sake, but for yours.

Be generous with your time, your compassion,
and, when you can, your money.

Don't try to fight your boss's ego with your
own. Picture him as a toddler with undeveloped
social skills—then breathe, and congratulate
yourself for being in better control of your
behavior than he is.

Learn to be financially wise. Abundance isn't just about how much money you earn, but also what you do (and don't do) with it.

Sometimes, taking time to plan seems like a waste of time. It isn't. Thinking before acting can help you identify possible problems and find ways to get around—or eliminate—them before they happen.

It's said that we're all in sales, and the first thing we sell is ourselves. Stop every once in a while and ask yourself, *Am I the kind of person I'd like to buy from?*

Be willing to shift your thinking when what
you're thinking isn't working.

Leave brief voice mail messages and ask to be
called back if there's more to discuss. A message
that's too long may not get the attention it
deserves.

Don't trade happiness for success.

Don't trade a job you love for one that just pays well.

Often people say they learned from a crisis that forced them into new thinking. Don't wait for a crisis. When your job or your life is more struggle than enjoyment, it's time for new thinking.

If you can't explain your idea in 30 seconds or less, wait until you can.

Practice friendly body language—smiling, nodding your head, leaning forward slightly when you talk. Practice at home in front of a mirror so it looks natural when you use it with others.

If you're looking for a job, do something toward getting one every day, and look for ways to make it fun.

Give yourself permission to not be perfect.

For three months, keep a list of every penny you spend. You'll be surprised at how much you spend on things that don't matter very much.

For three months, keep a list of everything you do at work and at home and how long it takes to do it. You'll be surprised how much time you spend on things that don't matter very much.

Always check—and double check—your facts. Keep a list of sources in case someone asks.

Don't be overly sensitive, but if a coworker says something rude to you more than once, speak up. Don't accuse her of being rude; instead, let her know how what she said makes you feel and that it's not okay.

Try to remember that you are fifty percent of all your relationships.

If your boss is fired or leaves and isn't replaced, you should start looking for another job.

Frequent interruptions are stressful and distracting, and they steal time from your main goals. Turn off message alerts. Avoid the temptation to check your email, news updates, the weather, and social networking sites more than once or twice a day.

Being positive isn't about denying that bad things happen; it's about choosing to put your attention on what helps you be optimistic, confident, and happy instead of what doesn't.

Go into every encounter with a positive attitude and relaxed body language. Others will sense your energy and relax themselves.

Understand and follow the rules of your company's health insurance program. Charges add up quickly, and if you haven't followed procedures, the insurance company may refuse to pay.

When you're stuck trying to make a decision, hush all the voices of logic (they're what's keeping you stuck), and ask yourself, *What feels like the right thing to do?* Then hush all the voices that tell you why you can't, and do it.

Yoga, Tai Chi, and Chi Gong (Qigong) can reduce stress while helping you get or stay in shape.

You may find it easier to honor a commitment
to exercise if you sign up for a class.

Ask your boss how you can improve and
what it would take for her to consider that you
have improved. Send her a memo listing the
improvement she's suggested, and set up a time
to check back in.

Struggle is a choice we make when we spend
more money than we can comfortably earn,
when we try to control everyone and everything
around us, or when we believe we should be
perfect and everybody else should be, too.
Choose to stop it!

Enter negotiations with the intent to be flexible, but know what you will and won't accept. Honor your boundaries kindly but firmly.

A new boss may have a new communication style. Take your clues from the way she talks to you. Is she all business, getting right to the point? Or is she warm, taking time to chat? Talk to her the way she talks to you.

Prioritize—plan your work schedule rather than starting to work on the file that's on top.

Don't take it personally if your great ideas don't excite your boss. Many things can be going on in the background that you don't know about.

Reevaluate your life frequently. Is it the life you want to live? If not, what do you need to change so it is? After you tell yourself all the reasons you can't make those changes, make a list of twelve changes you *can* make, and start making those.

Look around you: What's taking space in your life that you don't need or even notice anymore? Pass it along to someone who will see it as new.

As the world gets more challenging, workplace stress increases. If you have stress you can't eliminate, take advantage of EAP (Employee Assistance Program) services, or sign up for a stress management class. Make it a priority to relax and be happy.

Do challenging jobs during the time of day when you're most alert, and do routine jobs when you're not as sharp.

Focus on your goal, not on all the blocks you have to get through.

Be gentle. Listen. Laugh. Love.

Find three things you can appreciate about your boss or troublesome coworkers, and focus on them instead of the things you don't like.

Journal. Make lists. When thoughts are chasing themselves through your head like a herd of unruly kindergartners, get them out of your mind and onto paper.

If another company buys your company and it already has people who do what you do, it might be time to look for another job.

If you want to advance to the executive level in your company, work toward supervisory positions in departments directly linked to company profits such as product development or sales rather than support departments such as communications or security.

You can't get where you want to go until you're willing to leave where you are.

Screen your calls. Often, voice messages save time because people aren't tempted to chat.

Learn something new about your industry every month—even if you don't think it will ever matter.

Learn to recognize your boss's moods, and wait to make requests until she appears to have time to listen.

Consider that if life were fair, you'd probably have to give a lot of your stuff back.

Your mind creates stress, not your life. What you think about what happens is often more important than what happens.

Identify behavior habits you slip into that make you unhappy, uncooperative, or unsuccessful, and change them. Notice the stories you tell yourself just before you slip into unhelpful behavior habits, and change *them*.

Ask questions. Make sure you know someone's complaints before you try to explain them away.

Every day do at least one quick, low-priority task so you'll have a feeling of satisfaction from finishing something.

Sometimes it's a good idea to stop arguing and agree to disagree.

Let your boss know about your success. A weekly email with an update will remind him of your value, and you can use this time to ask questions.

Choose to learn from criticism. Call it something with less of a buzz, like feedback, thank the person, and honestly consider how it can be helpful.

It takes the same amount of time and energy to imagine yourself succeeding as it does to imagine yourself failing. Notice which is more fun.

People are more likely to help you if they believe you'd be willing to help them.

Be someone others can trust.

If you're giving a talk, go early to check seating, lighting, and sound. Get a feel for the room. Make sure the microphone works. Smile. "Own" the room before the first participants arrive.

You'll never have everything you want because your wants expand daily. Enjoy what you have now instead of being frustrated that you don't have more.

Make a short list of what you need to cover in a critical conversation. If you rely on your memory, you could overlook important points.

Notice how many of your decisions are based on what other people say, think, feel, and do and how many are based on your own inner guidance. Practice following your inner guidance.

Look at conflict as an opportunity to solve a puzzle. To solve a puzzle, you need to be able to see most of the pieces, not just the ones that seem an obvious fit.

If you're a supervisor, look for ways to motivate employees, not control them.

Speak up about your accomplishments to your networking contacts. They need to know about your skills and achievements so they can determine which leads to pass on to you.

Read books on investing before you think you have money to invest. You might be surprised how a little bit, invested consistently, can add up.

Don't tweet anything negative about your job, your boss, or your coworkers. And don't post anything negative about your job, your boss, or your coworkers on Facebook or other social networking sites.

Before you leave work, list three things, in order of importance, you need to do the following day.

Don't interrupt, even if you're sure you know
what the speaker is going to say.

Don't interrupt, even if you're sure that what
you want to say is more important.

Stop and think before you respond, especially
when you're angry, tired, hungry, excited,
confused, rushed, or stressed.

If an interviewer says you don't have enough experience in the industry you're trying to enter, ask what the most important aspects of the job are. Then describe how you were successful in those areas in your previous industry.

Dress as well as your best-dressed coworkers. Have fewer clothes if you need to, but make sure what you have makes you look your best.

If your boss pushes you to explain something but you're not quite sure how, ask for time so you can organize your thoughts.

Don't try to control the uncontrollable. If you've tried your best to change something and continually met resistance, ask yourself, *How important is the change?* If it's not extremely important, let it go. If it is, look for a new approach and try again.

You become what you practice most: grumpy, frustrated, dissatisfied or pleasant, confident, and happy.

Be the kind of coworker you'd like to spend five days a week with.

Treat yourself to a massage at least once a month. It doesn't just feel good; it's also good for you.

If someone doesn't understand, don't keep repeating yourself. Look for new words, break big ideas into several smaller ones, draw diagrams, and be creative looking for ways to show what you mean.

When choosing a job, consider how you want to *feel* at work as well as what you want to do.

Don't wait for your boss to ask for your side of
a conflict. Make an appointment, and calmly,
relaying facts, tell her.

If you're a boss, encourage truth from your
employees; you'll be more likely to learn about
little problems before they become big ones.

Before you tell others about your success, take
a moment to consider the steps you took to get
there so you can use them for your next project.

Working to have good relationships can make you happier than working to have more stuff.

In some companies, formal procedures must be followed exactly; in others, the policies serve as a guide until employees learn a way to streamline the process. Know which rule your company follows, and follow it, too.

Take your vacations. Studies show that employees who do are more effective than those who don't.

Unless it's part of your job description, don't focus on the problems at work.

Be prepared for tricky interview questions like, "Describe a disagreement you had with a boss and how you handled it," and, "Describe how you deal with a coworker/client you don't like very much."

When journalists write, they remember to answer their readers' question: *What's in it for me (WIIFM)?* Remember to answer the WIIFM question when you ask others to make a change.

Ask yourself frequently, *Is what I think helping me get where I want to go, or is it keeping me stuck where I don't want to be?*

If it's important for people to reach you by phone, ask a friend to call and see if your phone system or your staff makes it easy.

Don't frustrate your staff by expecting them to do what *you* would do if you were doing their job. Tell them the results you want, and encourage them to find the best way to accomplish those results.

Kindly, but firmly, ask people who want to take over or derail your presentation to please hold their comments until you're finished.

Build a strong network at work; who you know is often more important than what you know when management looks for someone to promote.

Be a team player, but know when to stay focused on your own projects, too.

Write down the suggestions and instructions
your boss gives you. If the information is
confusing, ask for clarification. Then send
an email outlining her request, and ask for
confirmation that you've understood correctly.

Reevaluate your goals frequently: Are they the
right ones? Are you doing the most effective
things you can do to reach them?

Don't assume the people you're talking to
know what you know. Ask, "Are you familiar
with…" before going into details.

To avoid confusion, explain one point at a time. Make sure your listener understands each point before you move to the next one.

Stay calm when others get upset. Instead of contributing to the problem, you might be able to help.

At some point you are probably as efficient as you're ever going to be. Let that be okay.

Ask for letters of recommendation before
you leave a job so you can hand a copy to
interviewers you want to impress.

Before you make a request, pitch a sale, or submit
a proposal, act as if you are the recipient. Read
your proposal as if you'd never seen it before.
Would the request, pitch, or proposal sell *you*? If
not, why not? Fix your request until you'd buy it.

Don't slip into victim mode at work or at home.
When something isn't going the way you want it
to, step back and figure out why. Then figure out
what you need to do to get the results you want.

When you're interviewing for a job, ask what
qualities your boss would like you to have. If
you'd be a good fit, tell the interviewer why.

Body language speaks louder than words. People
will trust how they feel about you more than
they will trust what you say.

Don't wait to do what you long to do until
you're "good enough." Jump in. You'll get good
enough with practice.

When others come to you for advice, avoid the temptation to rescue them. Instead, guide them with questions so they figure out the solution themselves.

If you want to sell an idea or a product, mirror your listener's body language. Match her breathing; adapt your tone of voice and speaking pace to hers. Use the sensory words she uses (think, hear, see, feel). People are more comfortable with people who seem like them.

Before you take someone's advice on how to be a success, look at how successful he is.

Update your to-do list every day. Don't risk overlooking an important deadline or waste mental energy trying to remember what you need to do.

If you need a response to your email, let recipients know you do and when you need it.

If you need to know that someone received your email, ask for a quick "got it" response.

Wait to take ideas to your boss until they're thought out: what you propose, how it benefits your boss, how you see it being done, what the drawbacks might be.

Being happy and successful doesn't just happen. Learn the relationship skills you need to be happy and successful.

During an interview, pay attention to how you feel with the person who will be your boss. The job description may sound wonderful, but if your boss is rude, impatient, insensitive, uncertain, unclear, or unethical, your dream job could be a nightmare.

If you suspect your accent or diction could keep
you from getting a promotion, take a class to
improve it. If you're not sure, ask your boss,
and make it comfortable for him to give an
honest answer.

Know the most important tasks to complete
each day, and avoid distractions that pull you
away from them.

You'll be happier in a career you're drawn to, at a
company you want to work for, than you will be
doing work other people insist is better for you.

A silent employee isn't necessarily a happy one. If you're a boss, find out if your silent employee wants to tell you something but is afraid.

When you ask for feedback, be quiet and listen. The moment you try to explain (or even start thinking about how you'll explain), you mentally close the door to any help the person you're asking might give.

If what you've been doing to solve a problem doesn't work, try something new. Almost anything will be more likely to work than continuing to do what hasn't worked so far.

Some of the people you work with may be crazy—or at least emotionally immature. Don't believe you can fix them. Instead, learn how to work with them or around them.

Find one thing to like about everyone you don't like very much, and think about that when you're working together.

Bosses appreciate and sometimes even reward employees who are positive and cooperative when policies and procedures change.

If you're feeling overwhelmed, list everything you think you need to do, rank the items by importance, and then focus on the tasks at the top of the list.

Bumper sticker wisdom: Don't believe everything you think.

Not everyone who asks for feedback wants the truth. Usually, it's wise to err on the safe side by not being *too* frank.

You'll be happier if you remember the difference between a problem and an inconvenience.

Sales is a numbers game; when you're looking for a job, you're selling yourself. Don't let yourself be discouraged. The more jobs you apply for, the closer you get to someone who will say yes.

Be your best self at work. People the boss doesn't like are the first to go when it's time for layoffs.

Before you start a new job, find out what
software you'll be using. If you don't know the
program, sign up online for a trial period so
you can become familiar with it.

At work, as in other games, you can only win if
you understand the rules. Understand the rules
where you work and stay in the loop.

Kindly, but firmly, interrupt an interrupter by
saying, "Excuse me; let me finish my
thought..."

Avoid having a desk or table between you and a person you want to connect with.

Let your boss share the credit for a project's success even if all she did was get out of your way. It helps if you can remember to enjoy the process of your work and not just the results.

If you don't work the traditional work schedule, post your hours at your workstation and leave them on your voice mail so others won't be frustrated trying to find you.

Each company has its own culture. You'll be happier if you know the dos and don'ts where you work and abide by them.

If you hate your job, do whatever it takes to find a new one.

Don't change who you are to make others happy. Notice that others aren't changing who they are to make *you* happy.

Ask someone you trust for feedback about
the way you talk: the tone, the pace, your
pronunciation, and even the words you use. Do
you sound strong, confident, open, informed?
If not, what do you need to change so you do?

If you're assigned to a team and you do most of
the work, send your boss regular updates. Keep
the tone informative, not judgmental.

You can't say "thank you" too often.

Dismissive comments, sarcasm, huffing, and eye rolling are only appropriate in junior high school.

You *will* make mistakes. Own them. Fix them. Try not to make the same ones again.

Don't hold grudges. After a conflict, take a break, breathe, and return as if nothing had happened.

When you're not sure what to do, make a list of twelve possibilities. Don't judge them; just put them on the list. Chances are, one idea will emerge as a good next step.

Learn the rules nobody tells you about by watching how other people are successful.

Ask yourself frequently, *What thoughts and behaviors have gotten me where I am at work and in life? What thoughts and behaviors do I need to change to help me get where I want to go? To be happy?*

Don't be a name dropper; it really doesn't impress anyone.

Check your company's policy before sending or accepting gifts from business associates outside your company.

Join your professional association, even if your employer won't pay for it. Go to meetings, and don't just talk to people you know. While it's important to nurture relationships, it's also important to begin new ones.

Be as kind as you can be to every living thing.

Being kind doesn't mean letting others take advantage of you. When you set boundaries and honor them, you're being kind to yourself.

Your cover letter is as important as your resume. Consult a career book on how to write cover letters, and make yours professional and easy to read.

Sometimes you need to leap before you're ready. Other times you need to wait until you've got your ducks in a row. Learn when to do each.

Don't make your boss prove she has more power than you.

Assume others are happy with their own religion. Work isn't the place to recruit people to yours.

Remember names. Say a new name when you're introduced. Then repeat it silently several times. Find a way to link the first letter of the name with the first letter of a feature or characteristic of the person. As soon as you can, write it down. Reread your list of names frequently.

Ask! The answer could be yes. Ask someone who can say yes. Ask as if you expect a yes.

Others who appear smarter may just be better actors.

Dress codes are more relaxed all the time, but understand that deep cleavage, multiple piercings, and tattoos may keep you from getting a job or a promotion.

Save yourself and others confusion: Date all documents and drafts with the current date.

Consider sending only a memo by email and the related files (especially long ones) by interoffice or regular mail.

Don't tease coworkers. Humor that makes anyone uncomfortable isn't funny.

A new boss wants to see who will be on his side. Don't go overboard, but do volunteer for assignments that are important to him that play to your strengths.

The best time to find a new job is before you leave your old one.

When you ask a question, don't supply the answer and ask if the listener agrees. Ask, and then pay attention to what she says.

Ask open-ended questions when you want to draw someone's thoughts out: What do you think about this project?

Ask closed-ended questions when you want a quick answer instead of a conversation: Are you ready for me to take the next step?

Read and understand your employee handbook. You may be bound by its policies regarding insurance plans, retirement benefits, dress codes, holidays, sick-leave pay, behavior, and dozens of other issues, and you need to know what they are.

Look for ways to feel good. When you feel good, you're more approachable, and people want to help you. When you feel good, your body creates chemistry that supports your immune system to keep you healthy.

Keep your dreams alive. Look for ways you can live them, instead of reasons you can't.

Avoid telling others how they should do their jobs.

If your email is longer than one screen, see if you can edit it. If not, send it as an attachment.

Deal with difficult people before your only option is to strangle them. Invite discussion to resolve conflict. Look for areas where you can agree. Look for ways to remember how unimportant they really are in your life.

How you say something—your body language, your tone of voice—is often more important than the words you use.

Ask yourself frequently, *What did I struggle with today? How can I get the results I want tomorrow without the struggle?*

Choose an email subject line that motivates the reader to open it: "Agenda for budget meeting" is better than "Budget meeting."

When more people contribute ideas, it's more likely a great idea will emerge. Make it safe for people you work with to contribute ideas.

When someone is being particularly annoying, try to picture him or her as a small child. This can help you soften your attitude and be a little less critical.

People are more inclined to help you when you seem in a good mood than when you're grumpy.

Your staff will be more likely to accept change if they have some input.

Most companies have a mission statement stating their goal and the way they intend to do business. It'll be easier for you to stay on track if you have one, too.

Don't send the same resume and cover letter to every potential employer. Use key words to reflect skills requested in the ad.

Since you can't always please everyone, think of reasons you are pleased with yourself.

When you're working with high energy and extreme focus, stop after 90 minutes in order to break the intensity. Walk around. Get a snack. Practice breathing meditation. Your next 90 minutes will be much more effective than if you hadn't taken a break.

Work for balance in your personality, relationships, experiences, and job responsibilities. The more balance you have in your life, the less stressed you'll feel when something goes wrong.

When making a presentation, look at your audience and smile before you start. Imagine the room is full of adoring fans.

Don't keep anything on your computer or in your desk drawers that you wouldn't want everyone to see. If you're ill, others may need access to your workspace.

Downplay drama—at work and at home.

Show respect for others whether you think they deserve it or not. You can't know what they've been through, what they're going through, or what their deepest fears are.

You'll probably forget a lot of this. Read the book again.